A Dare Too Far?

Written and Illustrated
by
Joanna Greenwood

ISBN: 9781724186881

To Anisha - With Best Wishes - Jo Greenwood
X

Guidance Notes can be found at the back of this book, for enabling use of the story to help with exploration and development of social skills.

Also available in the **Yew Tree Woodland Tales** series-

Book 1- New Kid on the Block by Joanna Greenwood
ISBN 9781549821547

Book 2- The Show-stopper by Joanna Greenwood
ISBN 9781980241522

Written with love for our beautiful British Wildlife, and hoping we can protect the precious creatures that have inspired these tales- including the humble hedgehog, whose numbers are so sadly dwindling.

Near Yew Tree Farm,
a small hedgehog
lived in a cosy, hollow log.

Always bored, she loved to roam,
and longed to venture far from home.
(Despite her being very small,
she seemed to have no fear at all!)

With two young sisters, she felt old;
and what to do, would not be told.

"Leave those berries—
they're for tea!"
her mum would say ...

But Hedgehog would just go ahead:
be scolded, and then sent to bed!

One morning though, as Hedgehog woke,
a friend's voice through her window spoke.

The magpie whispered in her ear-

There is a
playground far from here.
It is **the** best- I know the way.
We could both go
and play all day!

We'd need to
cross a road, of course.
I'll ask my mum
if you ask yours!

So, Hedgehog skipped off speedily
to beg her parents to agree ...

So off stomped Hedgehog, in a strop—
not wanting to return, nor stop ...

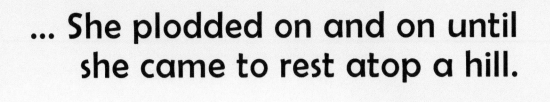

... She plodded on and on until
she came to rest atop a hill.

Down from a tree there, Magpie flew
and joined her to take in the view.

Magpie pointed with her wing-
in the distance was a swing ..

... But in-between, a road wound through.

At **that** sight Hedgehog's
fear now grew!

"I asked my parents- they said no!"
said Hedgehog, with her head held low.

"Let's show them we know best!" she cried.

It sounded good, so off they set,
until the long, smooth road they met.

Here, Hedgehog felt a bit more scared,
but carried on, as she'd been dared.

When suddenly,
from round a bend,
a truck sped
at our little friend!

Hedgehog rolled up tight inside
her coat of prickles, there to hide
and hope the truck passed overhead;
now wishing she had stayed in bed!

As the lorry rushed straight past,
the wind-gust spun her round so fast.
Left quite dizzy, she'd lost track-

she couldn't tell which path led back!

The roadside hedgerow
she squeezed through,
and hoped she'd
recognise the view.

She looked for
Magpie everywhere.
It seemed her friend
just did not care!

The bird did not
show up at all.
Our hedgehog felt
so lost and small.

She wandered off, hoping she might
find a way home, before midnight.
But everywhere looked just the same!

Then, as she sobbed, she heard her name ...

It wasn't Magpie's voice she'd heard;
instead, it was a wiser bird.

Kind Owl had seen her in distress.
She told him all about the mess ...

Both parents were in such a state,
when Hedgehog skulked-in quite so late!

Once Owl recounted
the close shave,
they shouted,
cried ...

... then hugs each gave.

At first, her sisters found it strange, but Hedgehog's scare had made her change.

Since then, she did as she was told- and cleaned up for the whole household!

Days later, Magpie finally
came round with an apology–

From that day on,
the friends **ALL** could
venture safely from their wood.

They laughed and played
among the trees ...

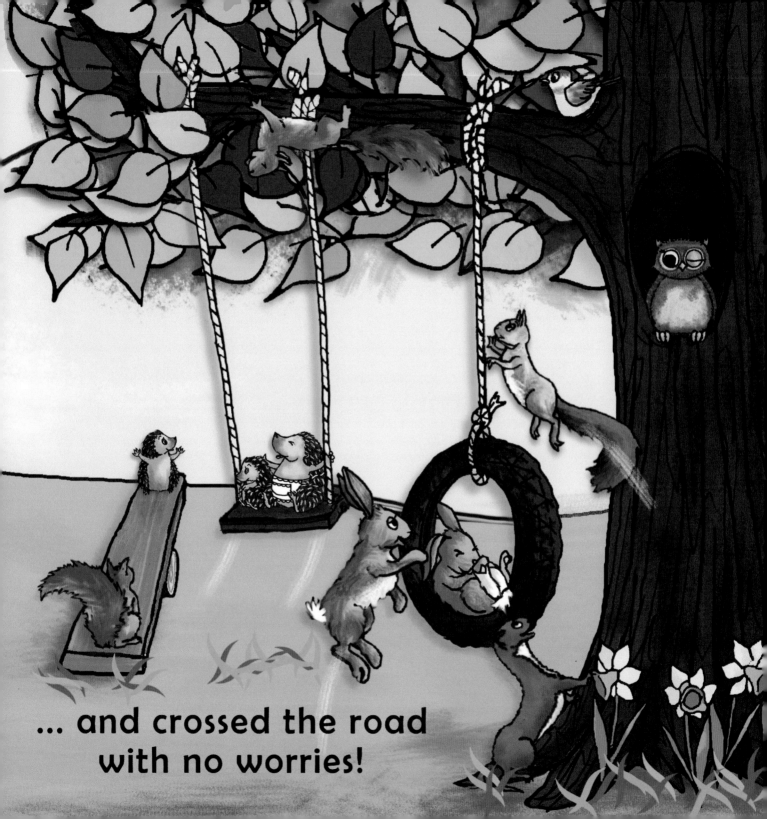

... and crossed the road
with no worries!

Information for Parents, Carers and Teachers

This story is designed to act as a discussion instrument for exploring social situations and behaviour choices with children, or for social skills development work.

It aims to tackle several moral dilemmas that are common when growing up, and which many find extremely tricky to understand or solve.

As well as encouraging conversation around general emotions displayed by the characters (both in the text, and within the illustrations), other issues touched upon within the tale are:-

Consequences of behaviour choices	**Correcting our mistakes**
Importance of listening to good advice	**Team work**
Respect for our elders	**Empathy for others**
Peer pressure	**Responsibility**
Danger of dares	**Road safety**
Friendship	**Hedgehog preservation (road tunnels)**

Individual readers will probably explain the characters' situations very differently, and may react (or may have already reacted) with many different feelings and actions- especially if they have already experienced similar circumstances in their own lives.

*The questions provided here serve merely as **optional tools for opening discussions**, and the answers are only **examples** of those possible. It may prove useful to hear how readers interpret the emotions shown, the choices made by the animals, and the consequences- or just how they describe the events in the pictures- especially if they differ from those given here or given by others.*

Asking "what might happen next?" before each page turn, often gives interesting answers.

Hopefully "A Dare Too Far!" can also prove valuable in helping gain an insight into an individual's thinking processes and social understanding and friendships, as well as being an endearing story in itself.

Suggested Discussion Questions

How does Hedgehog feel at the start of the story?
Bored/ wanting an adventure.
Frustrated/ cross/ annoyed she can't do what she wants.
She wants to be a grown-up.

What kind of things did she do that upset her family?
Didn't listen to instructions/ her parents.
Made a mess/ played with/ ate / damaged others' belongings, and wasn't sorry/ didn't care.
Acted a poor example to her little sisters.

How does Hedgehog feel when Magpie visits? Happy/ excited at the thought of an adventure.

What did her parents think of her idea of the playground trip?
Worried about the road, and Hedgehog getting hurt.
They say she can't go, as it is too unsafe and risky.

How did Hedgehog react?
She felt angry, ignored her parents and stormed off.

What silly things did Hedgehog do next?
Listened to Magpie and followed her dare, even though she was frightened and her parents had forbidden her.
Crossed the road, without looking/ listening both ways and checking it was clear first.

Was Magpie really the good friend Hedgehog thought she was? Why?
NO- She dared Hedgehog to go to the park and cross the road, even though she knew it was dangerous and against Hedgehog's family's wishes.
She flew off and left Hedgehog to cross the road alone.
She never waited for/ looked for Hedgehog, nor helped her home afterwards.

What else could have happened to Hedgehog?
She could have been hurt crossing the road; not found her way home; or got into more danger on the way home.

How did her parents feel when she returned?
Worried it had got so late/ what might have happened- and then relieved/ thankful/ happy to have Hedgehog back safe.
Cross that Hedgehog had ignored them; trusted and followed Magpie's dare; and crossed the road alone.
Cross with Magpie.
Grateful to Owl.

How did Hedgehog and Magpie try to help put things right?
Hedgehog apologised to her family, changed her ways and helped around the house more.
Magpie said sorry to her friend, and arranged the tunnel as a surprise, and to help all friends cross to the park.

Who could your "Owl" be in real life if you needed help? Teacher, Parent, Carer, Trusted Friend, etc.

What else may we have learned from the story? To think about other people's feelings, as well as our own; and to listen to good advice, especially from trusted grown-ups.

Printed in Poland
by Amazon Fulfillment
Poland Sp. z o.o., Wrocław